The Show Offey Seed

by Selia White

Illustrated by Glen Holman

The Showy Offey Seed

All rights reserved; no part of this publication may be reproduced or transmitted by any means, electronic, mechanical, photocopying or otherwise, without the prior written permission of the publisher.

Written by Selia White

Published by Selia White

Illustrations and book design by Glen Holman
www.glenholman.com

ISBN: 978-1-7396373-0-9

Copyright © 2022
The moral right of the author has been asserted.

The Showy Offey Seed

Dedication

I dedicate this book to my sister Sonia.
Who encouraged me to write.

Also to my little family unit.
Sister Marcia. Niece Sinead.
And my two Great nieces, Qamara and Amijah.

Also to my brother in law, Arn.

In a land where trees grew tall and strong.

Comes the true tale of the Showy Offey Seed.

On the coolest, coldest, crispest, crunchiest day,
the most elegant, elusive, extraordinary egotistical tree in the forest, lovingly released a seed.

The seed pirouettes to earth, spinning and spiralling and somersaulting.

Softly, soundlessly, spontaneously, surreptitiously, spreading, sprawling, shimmering and showering the air on his way to the rich, varied, magnificent floor of the forest.

On landing with great flourish and flare, flouncing and fussing, he was amazed, astounded and astonished that there was no welcoming ceremony gathered to acknowledge his most splendid, stupendous, startling, singular stunning arrival.

No brass band blaring, no bandsman on the bandstand blowing, no bunting.

No mayor, no march, no marvelling multitude, memorably musing at his melodramaticness.

Look at me! Look at me! Look at me!

I can turn like a top, tinkle on my toes, I can tumble, twisting and twirling, tipping and tapping

Without ever even getting near to tripping.

I am glorious to see.

How extraordinary it would be, if it is possible, I am glorious only to me

No one saw his magnificence, his majesty, his mystery, maintained maddeningly, monstrously merely a minute.

He mangled, mingled and merged, with the multitude of seeds mounted on the mossy mound, under the misty milky moonlight splashed splendid ground.

The Showy Offey Seed struggled, staggered, stumbled, and swayed, then swaggered to his feet.

Seeing seeds scatter, a slow, slanted, smirky, sly smile spread smugly across his face.

Sauntering, he said, I am so desperately sorry for you, that you are not me.

You will never know how good it feels to live in my shell.

I could weep for you I am so sad.

It must be wonderful for you to be in my presence.

I wish I was you, so I could experience it myself.

Look at me! Look at me! Look at me!

Am I not the most glorious, glamorous, gorgeous, glowing, grounded seed, you have ever seen?

Admire me at your leisure.

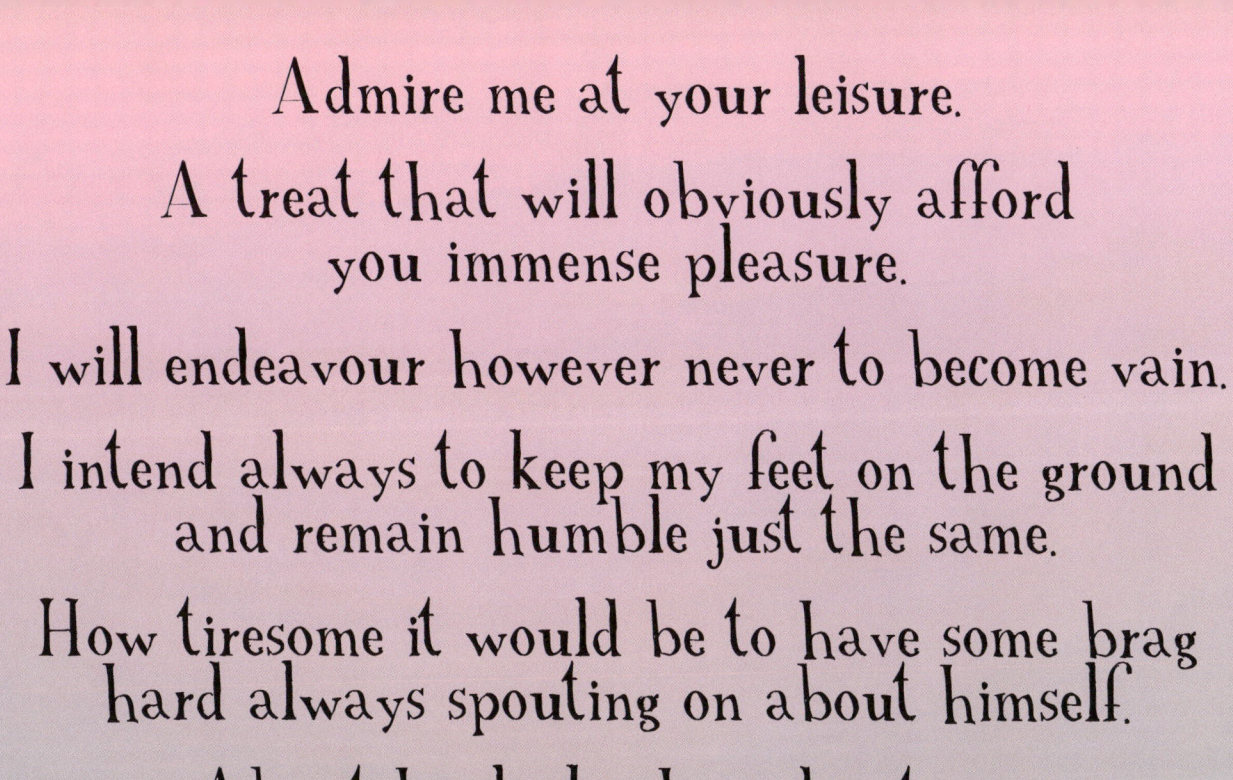

A treat that will obviously afford
you immense pleasure.

I will endeavour however never to become vain.

I intend always to keep my feet on the ground
and remain humble just the same.

How tiresome it would be to have some brag
hard always spouting on about himself.

About his looks, his adventures,
his clothes, his status, his wealth.

How sad that would be.

I'm so glad I can say with sincerity

You would never see such
behaviour in me.

I'm not a pretender when it comes to being magnificent.
When I say I am the best, I really am.
To be honest, I am actually better than best.
It's just that my modesty prevents me from boasting.
That I am in fact brilliant in most things.

The other seeds clasped their hands hard over their ears in an attempt to drown him out.

They tried to cover their eyes at the same time, so as not to have to see him.

But unfortunately two hands were insufficient for the task.

In desperation they started talking loudly amongst themselves.

But he only spoke louder himself.

How rude you all are he said, and selfish.

You talking, instead of listening to me.

Some seeds have absolutely no sense of priority.

Here I am giving of myself for your benefit, and this is how I am received.

If I was selfish I would stop talking and leave.

But Lucky for you, I do not possess a selfish bone in my body.

As I am sure you have perceived.

Imagine how your life would be if I had never arrived.

Unbeknownst to him, the other seeds were indeed imagining exactly that, with great enthusiasm.

They attempted to
roll away from him.

But he only rolled faster
and followed them.

Be careful, he snapped, you
almost left me behind.

Then you'd be sorry.

The other seeds were enormously sorry.

Their flushed, flustered, flummoxed, frustrated,
and, furious faces looked back at him in disbelief.

Cheer up he said you didn't lose me.

Just take more care in future.

Splendid specimens like me
don't grow on every tree.

I have often been told that I am unique and wondrous.

Mainly be myself, it is true.

But never the less it makes the fact no less valid a view.

The time was quickly approaching
for all good seeds to be planted.

Each chose a spot that looked suitable,
then instinctively burrowed down.

Minutes before they all disappeared down the
dark dank depths to their destiny, the Showy
Offey Seed began his final surmise.

I of course will be the splendour of the forest.

My leaves will be the greenest.

My branches will stretch the farthest.

My trunk will be the strongest.

My roots will be the longest.

Millions will marvel, mesmerized
at the marvellous, momentous, memorable,
miraculous monument of a tree.

That is me.

The earth was welcomingly warm and wormy.
Like a bespoke Mother Nature eiderdown.
The sun and the rain alternated in showering them each morning.

The seeds soon fulfilled their part in the nature play, and began to sprout green shoots.
All that is, except the Showy Offey Seed.

All his bombastic bragging and boasting had completely used up his entire supply of natural goodness contained within his shell.

His kernel was empty.

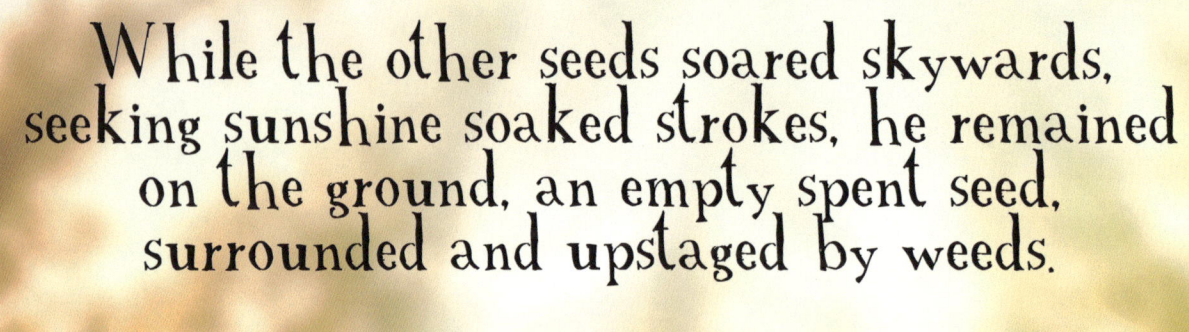

While the other seeds soared skywards, seeking sunshine soaked strokes, he remained on the ground, an empty spent seed, surrounded and upstaged by weeds.

In between the branches of the old established trees, swished by the wind, a barely audible voice was carried.

Look at me! Look at me! Look at me!

A faint, flat, faltering, whisper, from a feeble, forlorn, forgotten, Showy Offey Seed

Acknowledgements

To my family, friends and associates who encouraged, supported and helped me on my writing journey.

Without whose help I may have been floundering still.

Printed in Great Britain
by Amazon